The Cat in the Hat's Learning Library

To Viv and Charlie with love
—T.R.

The editors would like to thank
BARBARA KIEFER, Ph.D.,
Charlotte S. Huck Professor of Children's Literature,
The Ohio State University, and
DAVID GRIMALDI, Ph.D.,
Curator, Department of Entomology,
American Museum of Natural History,
for their assistance in the preparation of this book.

Visit us on the Web!
Seussville.com
randomhousekids.com

Educators and librarians, for a variety of teaching tools, visit us at
RHTeachersLibrarians.com

Library of Congress Cataloging-in-Publication Data
Rabe, Tish.
On beyond bugs! : all about insects / by Tish Rabe ; illustrated by Aristides Ruiz.
  p. cm. — (The Cat in the Hat's learning library)
Summary: Rhyming text and illustrations depict the Cat in the Hat and his friends exploring
the many different kinds of insects, their characteristics, and behavior.
ISBN 978-0-679-87303-7 (trade) — ISBN 978-0-679-97303-4 (lib. bdg.)
1. Insects—Juvenile literature. [1. Insects.] I. Ruiz, Aristides, ill. II. Title. III. Series.
QL467.2.R335 1999 595.7—dc21 98-51746

Printed in the United States of America
55 54 53 52 51 50 49 48

On Beyond Bugs!

by Tish Rabe

illustrated by Aristides Ruiz

The Cat in the Hat's Learning Library®

Random House 🏠 New York

I'm the Cat in the Hat,
and I'm glad that I found you.
Right now, if you look,
you'll see insects around you.

They live in the water,
the earth, and the sky.
Just wait...and you'll soon
see an insect go by!

There are millions of them.
I will show some to you.
Your mother will not
mind at all if I do.

Most insects you'll meet
have hard shells and lay eggs.

PRAYING MANTIS

BUTTERFLY

They have wings and can fly
and they all have six legs.

GRASSHOPPER

LADYBUG

BLACK ANT

Spiders aren't insects!
This news couldn't wait!
Instead of six legs,
every spider has eight!

If you look at an insect
up close, you will see
that its body's in parts
and each insect has three.

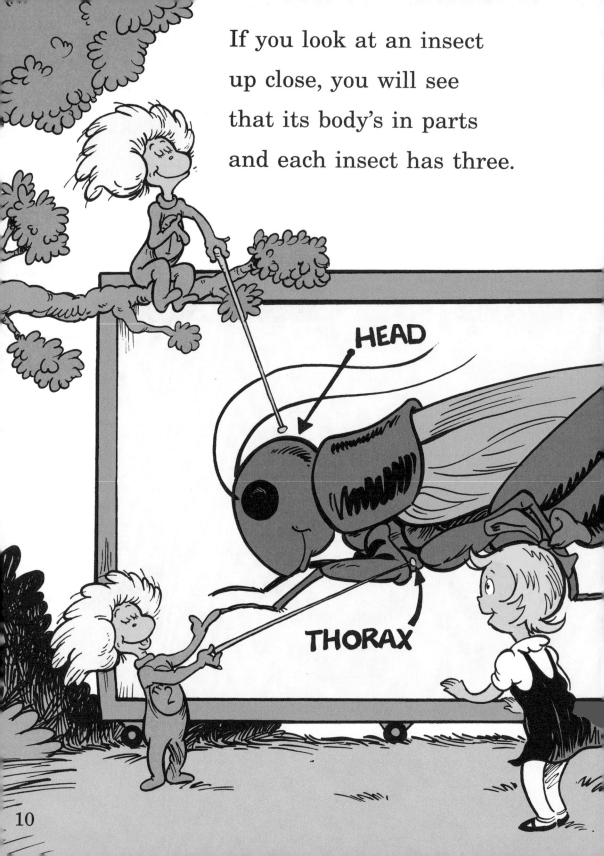

HEAD

THORAX

First the head, then the thorax,
and here at the end
is the longest part, which
is called: the abdomen.

ABDOMEN

CRICKET

Insects cannot see
all the things that surround them,
so they each have two feelers
to touch what's around them.

An insect has feelers on top of its head.

Some look a lot like a thin piece of thread.

While others look much more
like feathers instead.

We wish we had feelers,
but we don't have any.
You can also call feelers
by this name: "an-ten-ee"!

Watch an insect and see
all the things that it does.

Some can swim,

DIVING BEETLE

DOG FLEA

jump,

or crawl.

PIPEVINE CATERPILLAR

14

Others chirp,

CRICKET

flash,

FIREFLY

or buzz.

BUMBLEBEE

15

Birds and frogs look for insects in order to eat them.
So insects work hard to make sure they don't meet them.

Some, like this wasp,
have bright colors that say,
"Don't come near me! I'll sting you!
So just stay away!"

16

This moth's wings are colored to look like the tree it is resting upon so that no one can see it.

UNDERWING MOTH

This spittlebug sits
and he spits out a bubble.
It's wet and it's cool
and can save him from trouble.

For when he's all covered
in bubbly foam,
if a hungry bird comes,
it thinks...

nobody's home!

Here is a riddle
I learned from my mother.
How's a skunk and a ladybug
like one another?

When danger is near,
it is easy to tell—
they suddenly give off
a terrible smell!

These busy insects
are my friends, the ants.
They like to eat seeds,
other insects, and plants.

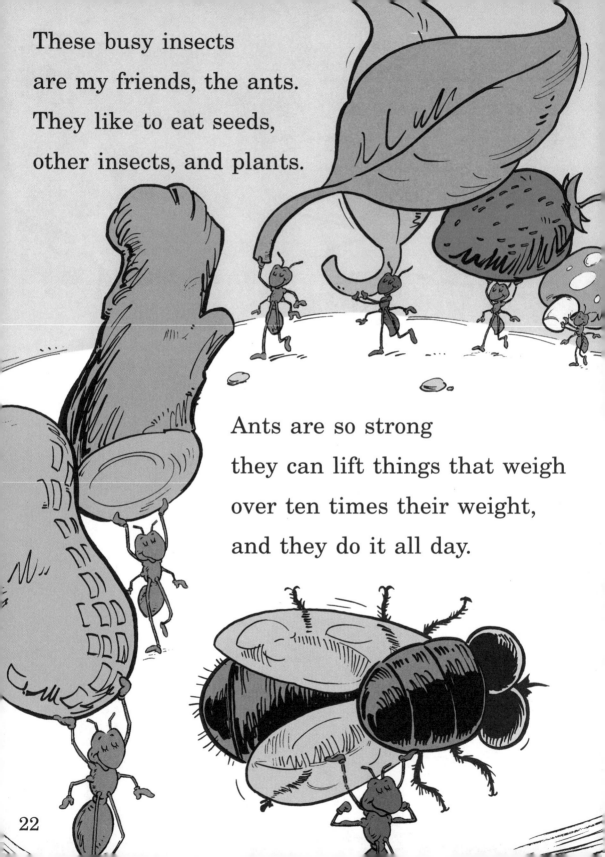

Ants are so strong
they can lift things that weigh
over ten times their weight,
and they do it all day.

So if you were as strong
as an ant, you would see
you could lift up ten cats
in tall hats...easily!

Watch these honeybees and
I am sure you'll agree
that these bees are as busy
as busy can be!

Worker bees collect food
and they keep the hive clean.
They protect it from danger
and wait on their queen.

She must stay in one place.
It is her job to lay
dozens and dozens
of eggs every day.

When a bee has discovered
where food can be found,
she goes back to her friends
and starts dancing around.

First she wiggles,

then waggles

in circles and so
all the other bees know
which direction to go.

We can grow lots of flowers
with help from the bees.
They store dust from each flower
in back of their knees.

This dust is called pollen.
Next flower they find—
when they land on it, they
leave some pollen behind.

This is called pollination
and it makes the new seeds
that grow even more flowers,
which everyone needs.

29

Some insects I know
can be unwanted guests.
Fleas, flies, and mosquitoes
can really be pests.

Fleas live on cats, dogs,
rats, hamsters, and mice.
Their bite is quite itchy,
which isn't too nice.

But they're wonderful jumpers.
Why, if we were fleas,
we'd jump over a house
and we'd do it with ease!

Have you ever wondered...

Why does a fly buzz?

Well...

It beats its wings fast,
and each time that it does,
its wings make a sound
you can hear in your ear,
and this sound lets you know
there's a fly flying near.

Here's a fact about flies
that we both thought was icky.
They can walk upside down,
since their feet are so sticky!

I don't think mosquitoes
are very polite.
When they're hungry, they land,
and they sting when they bite.

But it's only the female
mosquitoes that do.
Male mosquitoes will never
come bothering you.

Caterpillars do something
you might think is strange.
They start out as one thing,
then one day they change.
Some spin a small house
on a branch just like this,
and this home that they make
is called a chrysalis.

If you watch it, you'll see
when a few weeks go by,
it turns into a beautiful
new...butterfly!

Here's a quick fact
that we both thought was neat.
Butterflies can
taste their food...with their feet!

On warm summer evenings,
you may see the light
of fireflies flashing
off-on in the night.

They are like tiny flashlights
that float in the sky,
and if you want to catch them,
it's all right to try.

Use a jar with a lid.

Watch them glimmer and glow.

Then open the jar up...

and let them all go!

All day and all night,
on the ground, in the air,
insects are moving around
everywhere.

It's important for us
to keep learning about them.

The world that we know
couldn't go on without them.

The butterfly, ladybug, ant,
and the bee
make everything better...

for you...

and for me!

GLOSSARY

Abdomen: The third and last section of the body of an insect.

Chrysalis (say KRIS-a-lis)**:** The hard, unmoving stage between a caterpillar and a butterfly.

Hive: The place that bees live in.

Insect: A small animal with three pairs of legs and a body with an outer shell that is jointed and divided into three parts.

Pollen: A yellow, dust-like substance produced by flowers. It is carried by wind, birds, or insects to other flowers, where it forms seeds.

Pollination: The transfer of pollen from one flower to another.

Thorax: The part of an insect's body between the head and the abdomen. The wings and the legs are attached to it.

FOR FURTHER READING

Ant Cities by Arthur Dorros (HarperCollins, *Let's-Read-and-Find-Out Science®,* Stage 2). All about life inside an anthill—with instructions on how to make a simple ant farm! For kindergarten–grade 3.

Fireflies in the Night by Judy Hawes, illustrated by Ellen Alexander (HarperCollins, *Let's-Read-and-Find-Out Science®,* Stage 1). How fireflies live, make "cold" light, signal each other, and are used by people around the world. For preschoolers and up.

The Little Butterfly by Sherry Shahan (Random House, *Step into Reading®,* Step 2, A Science Reader). Photographs follow the life cycle of a monarch butterfly. For preschool–grade 1.

Monster Bugs by Lucille Recht Penner, illustrated by Pamela Johnson (Random House, *Step into Reading®,* Step 3, A Science Reader). All about the biggest and fiercest bugs in the world! For grades 1–3.

National Geographic Little Kids First Big Book of Bugs by Catherine D. Hughes (National Geographic Children's Books, *Little Kids First Big Books*). A photo-illustrated introduction to insects. For preschool–grade 3.

INDEX